The Taoist Priest of Laoshan Mountain

Adapted by Cao Zuorui
Illustrated by Du Dakai

FOREIGN LANGUAGES PRESS   BEIJING

First Edition   1984

ISBN 0-8351-1091-5

Published by the Foreign Languages Press
24 Baiwanzhuang Road, Beijing, China

Printed by the Nationalities Printing House

Distributed by China Publications Centre (Guoji Shudian)
P.O. Box 399, Beijing, China

Printed in the People's Republic of China

There lived in the city of Zichuan, Shandong Province, a gentleman named Wang Qi. His ancestors had been high officials in the royal court and had left the family large estates and a spacious residence.

His was a "scholarly family", possessing a library of ancient books.

In time, Wang and his brothers inherited the estates. Being gluttonous and lazy, they eventually sold all their land. "Riches and beautiful women will come from successful book learning," thought Wang. "I am determined to study hard, too."

After his first day of study, his back ached and his legs felt weak; after the second day, his head swam. Casting his book aside, he grumbled, "Alas! It is indeed no easy matter to make a name for oneself as a scholar!"

Then he remembered that it is often said that on Laoshan Mountain, by the eastern sea, immortals frequently appear. "Let me learn from the immortals," thought he. "If I can attain The Way, I'll have no trouble acquiring a high position and great wealth."

His relatives and friends exhorted and his wife entreated him not to go. But he was adamant. Shouldering his luggage, he started confidently on his journey. "I am resolved to learn some magical arts before I come back," he vowed.

In high spirits he hurried on his journey, fording rivers and crossing mountains, until, after a few days, he reached the foot of Laoshan Mountain.

He saw a Taoist temple amid the cloudy mists.

Overjoyed, he forgot his fatigue and, with renewed strength, ascended the peak quickly. As he neared the temple, it indeed appeared like a haunt of the immortals.

Entering the main hall, Wang saw a Taoist priest sitting in meditation on a rush mat. His long, flowing white hair and saintly appearance evoked a feeling of deep veneration in Wang.

Kneeling on the ground to kowtow repeatedly, Wang reverently besought the priest to take him on as his disciple. The priest opened his eyes to look at Wang, then closed them again without saying a word, whereupon Wang implored all the more earnestly.

"It's not that I don't want to take you as my disciple," said the priest. "But you're pampered — you can't stand the hardships here!" "I can, I can! I can stand any hardship," Wang pleaded.

At dusk the priest's numerous disciples returned to the temple. Wang bowed to each, and then stayed there with them.

Very early the next morning, the priest handed Wang an axe, and told him to cut firewood with the other disciples. Wang readily agreed.

Wang had never done such work at home. His hands became blistered, his feet swollen and he ached all over. But he set his teeth and persevered, thinking to himself, "To be a superior man, one must first endure great hardships. I will struggle on, undaunted by all difficulties!"

Day in and day out, for a month's time, he persisted in cutting firewood, a task that grew more and more unbearable to him. He felt it would be better to return home. Secretly he decided to sneak down the mountain early the next morning.

On the evening of that day, when he returned to the temple, he saw the priest drinking with two friends. It was already quite dark inside the main hall.

The priest, instead of telling his disciples to light a lamp, cut a circular piece of white paper with a pair of scissors. He stuck the paper on the wall.

Instantly the white paper became a moon that illuminated the hall. It was so light that people's beards and eyebrows could be seen clearly, and it was so strange that Wang was transfixed with amazement.

The disciples stood at the side in attendance upon their teacher. "As the moon is so bright tonight and we are in high spirits," said one of the guests, "we ought to enjoy ourselves."

The priest nodded in consent. The guest took up a wine kettle and poured wine for all the disciples, saying, "Drink as much you can. Your teacher has agreed that today you can drink to your hearts' content."

Again Wang thought to himself, "Such a small kettle cannot hold enough wine to fill each person's cup. How can each drink his fill?" He hastily grabbed a large cup and held it out to be filled, fearing that the wine would soon be exhausted.

But the small kettle contained an inexhaustible supply of wine, which did not diminish even though every disciple drank three large cups. Again Wang was puzzled.

Meanwhile the other guest said, "In drinking wine and enjoying the moonlight, our happiness is still incomplete; it would be better to invite Chang'e down here to sing and dance and liven things up."

Having said this and not waiting for the priest to reply, the guest picked up a chopstick and threw it at the moon.

To almost everyone's amazement, a miniature and beautiful woman stepped forth from the moonbeams.

At first she was less than a foot high, but she soon grew to an ordinary height. With rings and pendants jingling and jewels resplendent, she was indeed like Chang'e descending into the world.

Lissom and graceful, Chang'e performed the exquisite "Rainbow Skirt and Feather Jacket Dance".

While dancing, she sang beautifully, "To be a goddess? Or to return to the world? Or to remain lonely and cold in the palace of the moon?"

After singing, she danced in a big circle, and then suddenly flew onto the table.

The people who were drinking were shocked. How could Chang'e be allowed to alight on the table! Just as they were about to stop her, she fell on the table with a clatter, becoming a chopstick once more.

The priest and his two guests laughed heartily, the disciples marvelled and Wang was stupefied with wonder.

After a while the two guests stood up and said, "We're so happy today, and we've drunk much wine. How about drinking in the palace of the moon before we part?" The priest nodded in assent.

The priest and his guests then moved their feast into the moon.
Viewed from below, they sat in the moon drinking and chatting
cheerfully. Their eyebrows and beards could be seen distinctly in
the moonlight, like images in a mirror.

As Wang stared spellbound, the moon gradually dimmed and went out. By the light of a candle brought by a disciple, he now saw only the old priest sitting in meditation on a rush mat. The two guests had vanished into thin air.

Raising his head, the priest asked, "Have you all had enough wine?" The disciples answered that they had. "In that case, you can all go to bed," the priest said. "Don't be late for woodcutting tomorrow morning." They obeyed.

Back in his room, Wang thought, "Our teacher indeed has great magical powers. If I could learn his magical arts, I would be ever-victorious when I leave this mountain." So thinking, he dropped his idea of going home.

Wang cut firewood every day for another month. He found this so hard that he could not stand it any longer. But the priest still did not teach him any of his magical arts, so Wang decided to raise the issue with the priest.

The next day he waited until the other disciples had gone woodcutting and then said to the priest, "I've come several hundred li from my home to be your disciple. Why should I always cut firewood? To be explicit, your humble disciple has never done such heavy work before. How much longer must this last?"

The priest smiled and said, "I knew you could not stand the hardship. Well, I'll send you home tomorrow." On hearing this, Wang pleaded, "Your disciple has worked hard for months. Even if I'm not good enough to learn the secret of immortality, you can still teach me some minor arts!"

    Instead of declining, the priest asked what he wanted to learn. After some reflection, Wang replied, "I've often noted that when you walk, walls are no obstruction. If you teach me how to walk through walls, I'll be well content!"

The priest agreed to his request and taught him the formula for passing through walls. With his face wreathed in·smiles and his eyes shining, Wang was filled with elation.

After Wang recited the formula, the priest told him to enter the wall. Wang faced the wall, his heart thumping, but he dared not walk at it as the priest instructed him to do.

Falteringly, Wang walked up to the wall, but stopped when he found it was still solid stone. He was sadly disappointed.

"You didn't do it right," the priest told him. "You have to lower your head and rush at the wall to pass through it." Standing several paces from the wall, Wang braced himself, lowered his head and charged at it.

Strange to say, as Wang dashed at it, the massive stone wall turned to vapour, and when he opened his eyes again he found himself on the other side. Wang was beside himself with joy.

Wang hastened in to thank the priest and inform him of his intention to return home. The priest warned him, "This art is to be used only in an emergency. Don't use it in doing wrong and don't brag about it; otherwise it won't work."

Wang hurriedly packed his luggage, and said farewell to his
teacher. The priest, saying no more, gave him some money for the
journey home and sent him down from the mountain.

Leaving the Laoshan Mountain behind, Wang sped joyfully home. His teacher's parting advice was already forgotten.

Back home, his first words to his wife were, "I've met an immortal and learned magical arts from him. Now walls are no obstacle to me, no matter how hard they may be." Face beaming, Wang was very pleased with himself.

But his wife did not believe him. "You don't believe me? I'll show you at once!" Wang said with full assurance. And then he added, "Go and fetch all our neighbours. Let them see that I am no ordinary mortal."

Many of the neighbours crowded around. Wang took off his hat and handed it to his wife. He drew back a few paces, recited the formula, lowered his head and dashed at the wall.

His head hit the hard wall, and sent him sprawling to the ground. When his wife and neighbours ran over to him, they saw that he had a swelling as big as an egg on his head.

His wife tittered and his neighbours roared with laughter.
Face crimson, his hand covering his head, Wang wailed in pain.
Then he cursed the "ungrateful old priest"!

劳山道士

曹作锐　改编

杜大恺　绘画

＊

外文出版社出版

（中国北京百万庄路24号）

民族印刷厂印刷

中国国际书店发行

（北京399信箱）

1984年（20开）第一版

编号：（英）8050—2339

00240　（精）

00140　（平）

88－E—251